Praise for Build and Monetize Chatbots: Build Chatbots, Create Apps, and Achieve Profit Potential

"A comprehensive guide for anyone looking to capitalize on the chatbot revolution. This book doesn't just teach you how to create chatbots—it shows you how to make them profitable. A must-read for entrepreneurs and business owners alike!"
— **Tim Ferriss**, Author of *The 4-Hour Workweek*

"This is the playbook for building a chatbot empire. From ideation to monetization, it's the ultimate resource for turning AI-driven conversation into real revenue. Highly recommended for anyone in tech or business!"
— **Gary Vaynerchuk**, Author of *Crushing It!*

"An essential guide that seamlessly integrates cutting-edge AI technology with practical business insights. If you're ready to turn your chatbot ideas into a successful business, this book is your roadmap."
— **Neil Patel**, Digital Marketing Expert & Author of *Hustle*

"A brilliant, step-by-step blueprint that takes you through every stage of chatbot development and monetization. This book will help you unlock new levels of success with AI-driven business models."
— **Marie Forleo**, Author of *Everything is Figureoutable*

"An invaluable resource for anyone serious about turning chatbots into a thriving business. This book brings together technical know-how with real-world strategies to help you maximize the potential of AI."
— **Chris Brogan**, Author of *Trust Agents*

"If you want to not only build chatbots but also turn them into profitable assets, this book is a game changer. Full of actionable insights and expert advice, it's an indispensable tool for entrepreneurs."
— **Sophia Amoruso**, Founder of *Nasty Gal* and Author of *#GIRLBOSS*

"Chatbots are the future of business, and this book teaches you how to harness that future to build lasting success. A must-read for anyone looking to stay ahead in the AI-driven economy!"
— **Simon Sinek**, Author of *Start with Why*

BUILD AND MONETIZE CHATBOTS

Build Chatbots, Create Apps, and Achieve Profit Potential

Maximilian Ford

Copyright © 2024 Maximilian Ford
All rights reserved.

No part of this book may be reproduced, distributed, or transmitted in any form or by any means, including photocopying, recording, or other electronic or mechanical methods, without the prior written permission of the publisher, except in the case of brief quotations embodied in critical reviews and certain other noncommercial uses permitted by copyright law.

Published by Ford Publishing
1234 Main Street, Suite 101
New York, NY 10001
www.fordpublishing.com

ISBN: 978-1-23456-789-0
Printed in the United States of America

Disclaimer
This book is for informational purposes only. The author and publisher make no representations or warranties regarding the accuracy or completeness of the information contained in this book. The author and publisher are not liable for any errors or omissions or for any outcomes resulting from the use of the information presented herein.

Trademark Acknowledgment
All product names, trademarks, or other references to products, services, or companies mentioned in this book are the property of their respective owners. All rights reserved.

Chapter 1: What Are Chatbots? _____ 8

The History of Chatbots _____ 9

Significance of Chatbots in Modern Business, Customer Service, and Daily Life _____ 12

Benefits and Potential Challenges of Chatbots _____ 15

Chapter 2: Getting Started: Tools and Platforms for Building Chatbots _____ 18

Tools and Platforms for Building Chatbots _____ 20

How to Choose the Right Platform _____ 24

Step-by-Step Instructions for Setting Up a Basic Chatbot ____ 26

Overcoming Common Beginner Challenges _____ 28

Chapter 3: Designing Chatbots That Engage and Convert _ 30

The Importance of Conversational Design _____ 31

Best Practices for Crafting Effective Conversational Flows ___ 32

Strategies for Personalizing User Experiences _____ 36

Tips for Improving Chatbot Usability _____ 37

Testing Chatbot Performance for Better Results _____ 39

Case Studies: Examples of Engaging and High-Converting Chatbots _____ 40

Chapter 4: Advanced Features: Enhancing Chatbots with GPT-4 and AI Tools _____ 42

GPT-4 and NLP Integration _____ 44

GPT-4 for Multi-Lingual Support _____ 47

Practical Steps for Implementing Multi-Lingual Features ____ 47

GPT-4 and Cross-Platform Integration _____ 49

Practical Steps for Implementing Cross-Platform Compatibility
_____ 49

Content Generation _____ 50

Personalized Recommendations _____ 51

Chapter 5: Monetization Strategies for Chatbots _____ 53

How Chatbots Generate Leads _____ 55

How Chatbots Drive Sales _____ 56

Examples of Sales-Boosting Chatbots _____ 57

How Subscription Models Work with Chatbots _____ 58

How Chatbots Implement Upselling and Cross-Selling _____ 60

Examples of Upselling and Cross-Selling Chatbots _____ 60

Examples of Chatbots with Paid Features _____ 62

Chapter 6: Developing Apps Around Your Chatbots _____ 64

What are APIs? _____ 69

Benefits of API Integrations _____ 70

Chapter 7: Scaling and Succeeding: Building a Chatbot Empire _____ 75

CHAPTER 1: WHAT ARE CHATBOTS?

A **chatbot** is a software application designed to simulate human conversation through text or voice interactions. By using **natural language processing** (NLP) and **machine learning** algorithms, chatbots understand and respond to user queries in a manner that mimics human conversation. These bots can be simple, rule-based systems that follow predetermined scripts, or they can be sophisticated AI-powered solutions that learn and adapt over time.

At their core, chatbots are built to assist, inform, and engage users, enhancing the efficiency of communication. They are often deployed on messaging platforms, websites, mobile apps, and even within customer service operations to provide immediate assistance, automate repetitive tasks, and improve user experiences.

The History of Chatbots

The evolution of chatbots is deeply tied to the advancement of artificial intelligence and natural language processing. The first significant milestone in chatbot development was **ELIZA**, a program created in 1966 by Joseph Weizenbaum, a computer scientist at MIT. ELIZA simulated conversation by recognizing keywords and applying pattern-matching rules to generate responses. Though rudimentary, it provided a glimpse of what could be achieved with human-computer interaction.

Following ELIZA, chatbots like **PARRY** (developed in 1972 by psychiatrist Kenneth Colby) introduced more advanced features, including simulating the behavior of patients with mental disorders, a feature that mimicked human-like conversation in a more complex manner. However, early chatbots were limited by their programming and often couldn't understand or engage in nuanced discussions.

The real shift toward the more sophisticated chatbots we see today began in the early 2000s with the advent of **machine learning** and **artificial intelligence** techniques. With the release of **Siri** by Apple in 2011, followed by **Amazon's Alexa** and **Google Assistant**, the chatbot industry saw a massive leap forward. These voice-activated assistants were designed not just to answer basic questions but to help users interact with their smartphones and home devices in a more conversational way.

More recently, **OpenAI's GPT-3** and **GPT-4** have revolutionized chatbot technology, allowing for more natural, context-aware conversations. These models can generate text that mimics human thought patterns and conversational styles with remarkable accuracy, making them ideal for complex tasks, from providing customer support to offering personalized recommendations.

How Have Chatbots Evolved?

Chatbots have evolved from simple text-based applications to sophisticated conversational agents powered by cutting-edge AI. Here's a closer look at the stages of evolution:

1. **Rule-Based Systems (1960s–2000s)**
   Early chatbots operated on scripted responses and pre-programmed rules. They lacked the ability to understand or learn from their interactions, relying entirely on a set of fixed

responses. This made them limited in scope and often frustrating for users. However, these bots were useful for simple tasks like answering FAQs or providing basic information.

2. **AI-Powered Chatbots (2010s)**
With the advent of AI, chatbots began to leverage machine learning and natural language processing to engage in more dynamic conversations. These bots could understand context, detect user intent, and provide personalized answers. Technologies like **intent recognition** and **entity extraction** allowed chatbots to go beyond scripted interactions, making them far more flexible.

3. **Conversational AI (2020s and Beyond)**
The latest evolution in chatbots is driven by large language models like GPT-3 and GPT-4. These models are capable of generating human-like responses, understanding context over longer conversations, and even engaging in emotional tone detection. Modern chatbots can perform tasks like scheduling meetings, providing detailed product recommendations, and assisting with technical support, often with minimal human intervention.

4. **Voice Assistants and Multimodal AI**
Voice-driven chatbots, such as Amazon's Alexa, Google Assistant, and Apple's Siri, have become integral parts of modern households and smartphones. These systems allow users to control smart devices, set reminders, and search for

information purely through voice commands. Furthermore, **multimodal AI**—the ability to process both text and voice inputs—has led to even more sophisticated and natural chatbot interactions.

Significance of Chatbots in Modern Business, Customer Service, and Daily Life

Chatbots have become a cornerstone of modern business strategies, playing a critical role in automating tasks, improving customer service, and driving efficiency. They offer tangible benefits to businesses, consumers, and employees alike.

1. Customer Service and Support

One of the primary applications of chatbots is in **customer service**. Businesses use chatbots to handle customer inquiries, provide technical support, and resolve issues without the need for human intervention. This significantly reduces wait times, provides customers with immediate assistance, and lowers operational costs for companies.

For example, **Sephora**, a global cosmetic retailer, uses a chatbot named **Sephora Virtual Artist** to guide customers through the makeup-buying process. The bot can analyze the customer's preferences, suggest products, and even recommend tutorials, creating a seamless shopping experience. This improves customer satisfaction and helps the business retain clients.

Moreover, chatbots can handle high volumes of inquiries at any time of day, allowing businesses to offer **24/7 customer service**. This is especially important in industries like **banking** and **telecommunications**, where customers may need assistance at unconventional hours.

2. Sales and Marketing

Chatbots are also heavily utilized in **sales and marketing**. They can be integrated into websites and social media platforms to qualify leads, recommend products, and even guide customers through the purchasing process. Many businesses have found that chatbots can dramatically increase conversion rates by making interactions more personalized and direct.

For instance, **Macy's** has integrated a chatbot into their app that helps customers find products, check out, and track orders—all in one place. The chatbot not only serves as a personal shopping assistant but also provides targeted promotions based on customer behavior.

3. Personal Assistance and Daily Life

On a personal level, chatbots have become integral to our daily lives through **virtual assistants** like Siri, Alexa, and Google Assistant. These bots help users perform everyday tasks such as setting alarms, sending messages, playing music, or controlling smart home devices. Their ability to integrate seamlessly into daily routines has made them indispensable to many users.

For example, **Google Assistant** helps users manage their calendars, send text messages, and even provide traffic updates, making it easier to stay organized throughout the day.

4. Healthcare and Mental Health

The healthcare industry is also benefiting from chatbots, particularly in terms of **mental health support** and **patient management**. AI-powered bots can act as the first point of contact for patients, offering advice, answering health-related queries, and even providing therapy sessions.

Woebot is a popular chatbot in the mental health space. It helps users cope with stress, anxiety, and depression by offering Cognitive Behavioral Therapy (CBT) techniques. Woebot uses conversational AI to help users reframe their thoughts and manage emotions, offering 24/7 support without the need for human intervention.

5. E-commerce and Retail

In e-commerce, chatbots help to personalize shopping experiences. For example, **H&M** uses a chatbot named **Ada** to suggest clothing styles based on customers' preferences, size, and past purchases. By doing so, the chatbot creates an intuitive and personalized shopping experience, increasing the likelihood of a sale.

Real-World Examples of Successful Chatbot Implementations

- **Bank of America's Erica**: Erica is a virtual assistant that helps Bank of America customers manage their finances. From checking balances to providing personalized financial advice, Erica streamlines banking tasks. Since its launch, Erica has become a crucial part of the bank's customer service model, handling millions of interactions and improving customer satisfaction.

- **Lufthansa's Chatbot, Mildred**: Lufthansa introduced Mildred to assist customers in booking flights, checking in, and receiving flight information. The chatbot has successfully reduced the need for human agents, freeing up customer service representatives for more complex queries.

- **Domino's Pizza's Pizza Bot**: Domino's introduced an AI-powered chatbot that allows customers to order pizza directly through Facebook Messenger, Twitter, and its website. This chatbot can remember previous orders, making reordering effortless, and it helps customers find locations and deals with ease.

Benefits and Potential Challenges of Chatbots

Benefits:

- **Cost-Effective**: By automating tasks traditionally handled by humans, chatbots reduce operational costs. Businesses can scale customer service without hiring additional staff.

- **Increased Efficiency**: Chatbots can handle multiple queries simultaneously, reducing wait times and providing immediate responses to users.

- **Personalization**: Chatbots can tailor interactions based on user preferences, enhancing the customer experience and driving conversions.

- **Availability**: Chatbots are available 24/7, ensuring that users can always get help, no matter the time of day.

- **Data Collection**: Chatbots can collect valuable data on user preferences, behaviors, and feedback, which can be used for improving products and services.

Challenges:

- **Complexity**: While modern chatbots are highly capable, developing and maintaining sophisticated AI models can be resource-intensive.

- **User Experience**: If not designed properly, chatbots can frustrate users, especially if they fail to understand context or provide inaccurate information.

- **Security and Privacy**: As chatbots handle sensitive data, businesses must ensure that proper security measures are in place to protect users' personal information.

Chatbots have come a long way from their humble beginnings, evolving into powerful tools that are shaping the future of business, customer service, and daily life. From enhancing customer experiences to driving sales, chatbots are revolutionizing the way we interact with technology. Understanding their development, capabilities, and potential is essential for anyone looking to innovate or profit in the rapidly growing AI industry. As businesses and individuals continue to adopt AI, chatbots will undoubtedly play an even more significant role in driving innovation and success in the years to come.

CHAPTER 2: GETTING STARTED: TOOLS AND PLATFORMS FOR BUILDING CHATBOTS

In the ever-evolving world of technology, chatbots have emerged as powerful tools for automating customer service, sales, and marketing tasks. Whether you are an entrepreneur, a developer, or someone interested in AI, understanding how to create a chatbot is an essential skill in the modern digital landscape. Fortunately, building a chatbot no longer requires deep coding knowledge. Thanks to the rise of **no-code** and **low-code platforms**, anyone can design, deploy, and manage a chatbot, even with little to no programming experience.

This chapter will walk you through the process of getting started with chatbot development. We will cover a variety of tools and platforms available for creating chatbots, explore how to select the right platform based on your goals and skill levels, and provide step-by-step instructions for building a simple chatbot. Additionally, we will compare popular chatbot platforms like **ChatGPT**, **Dialogflow**, and **Rasa**, highlighting their strengths and weaknesses. By the end of this chapter, you'll have the knowledge to begin your chatbot journey confidently.

Tools and Platforms for Building Chatbots

The first step in creating a chatbot is choosing the right development platform. Depending on your goals and technical expertise, there are several types of platforms available:

1. **No-Code Platforms**

   No-code platforms are designed for users with little to no programming skills. These platforms provide a visual interface where you can create chatbots by dragging and dropping components, making it easy for beginners to get started. No-code tools are ideal for simple chatbots focused on basic functions like answering FAQs or collecting contact information.

   Popular No-Code Platforms:

   - **Chatfuel**: Chatfuel is one of the most widely used no-code platforms for building Facebook Messenger chatbots. It offers a user-friendly interface, pre-built templates, and integration with various services like Google Sheets, Zapier, and more. Chatfuel is an excellent option for beginners who want to create simple chatbots for social media platforms.

   - **ManyChat**: ManyChat specializes in building bots for Facebook Messenger but has expanded to support SMS and email as well. The platform provides an intuitive drag-and-drop interface, allowing users to create automated workflows, broadcast messages, and track analytics.

- **Tars**: Tars allows users to create chatbots for websites and landing pages. Its drag-and-drop builder simplifies chatbot creation and is designed for users with no technical expertise. Tars is ideal for businesses looking to create lead-generation chatbots or optimize customer support.

2. **Low-Code Platforms**

Low-code platforms are more powerful than no-code platforms and allow for greater customization. These platforms provide a mix of visual tools and coding options, making them suitable for users with some programming knowledge. Low-code platforms are ideal if you want to create more sophisticated chatbots, such as those that require integration with other software systems or custom features.

Popular Low-Code Platforms:

- **Dialogflow**: Developed by Google, Dialogflow is one of the most popular low-code platforms for building chatbots. It uses natural language processing (NLP) to understand user input and respond intelligently. Dialogflow supports a wide range of platforms, including Google Assistant, Slack, Facebook Messenger, and more. It's perfect for those looking to create conversational bots with deeper integrations and advanced features.

- **Rasa**: Rasa is an open-source platform that offers high levels of customization and flexibility. Unlike no-code platforms, Rasa requires coding skills, but it provides powerful tools for building context-aware chatbots. Developers can use Rasa to create chatbots with machine learning capabilities, enabling the bots to improve over time based on user interactions. Rasa is ideal for developers looking to build complex, enterprise-grade chatbots.

- **Microsoft Bot Framework**: This framework provides a set of tools and services for building intelligent bots. It supports multiple programming languages, including C#, Node.js, and Python, making it a good choice for developers familiar with these languages. Microsoft Bot Framework integrates easily with Azure and allows you to deploy bots across various channels.

3. **AI-Powered Platforms**

   AI-powered platforms allow for even more sophisticated chatbot development. These platforms use machine learning, NLP, and sometimes even deep learning to create highly intelligent bots capable of understanding complex queries, learning from interactions, and adapting to user preferences.

Popular AI-Powered Platforms:

- **ChatGPT**: OpenAI's ChatGPT is an AI model capable of holding dynamic, human-like conversations. ChatGPT can be integrated into various applications, including customer service chatbots, content creation bots, and more. While not a traditional chatbot builder, it's widely used to create conversational agents with advanced language capabilities. Developers can fine-tune the model or use the GPT-3 API for more specific tasks.

- **IBM Watson Assistant**: IBM Watson is an AI-powered platform that uses machine learning to understand and respond to customer queries. Watson Assistant allows users to create advanced chatbots that can handle complex tasks, such as providing personalized recommendations and integrating with other business systems. The platform offers both no-code and low-code options, making it suitable for a wide range of users.

How to Choose the Right Platform

With so many chatbot-building tools available, how do you select the best one for your needs? Below are key factors to consider when choosing a platform:

1. **Your Skill Level**

    o   If you have no coding experience and need to build a simple chatbot, **no-code platforms** like **Chatfuel** or **ManyChat** will be the easiest to use.

    o   If you have some programming knowledge and want more flexibility and customization, **low-code platforms** like **Dialogflow** or **Rasa** will give you the ability to integrate advanced features.

    o   If you're an experienced developer or want to build highly intelligent bots, consider platforms that offer AI-driven solutions, such as **ChatGPT** or **IBM Watson Assistant**.

2. **Type of Chatbot**

    o   **Customer Service Chatbots**: If your goal is to create a customer service chatbot, you'll want a platform that specializes in NLP and can understand user queries in a conversational manner. Platforms like **Dialogflow, IBM Watson,** and **Rasa** are great options.

- **Lead Generation and Sales Chatbots**: For bots focused on generating leads and automating sales, no-code platforms like **ManyChat** or **Tars** can help you build simple yet effective bots quickly.

- **E-commerce Chatbots**: If you're building a chatbot for an e-commerce platform, look for platforms that can integrate easily with your store. **Shopify** offers chatbot integrations, and **ManyChat** can connect to various e-commerce platforms as well.

3. **Integration with Other Tools**

    - Make sure the platform you choose integrates with the tools you're already using. For instance, if you're using **Google Sheets** for data management, **Chatfuel** integrates seamlessly with it. Similarly, if you use **Slack** or **Facebook Messenger**, platforms like **Dialogflow** offer built-in integrations for those channels.

4. **Budget**

    - Consider the pricing models of each platform. **No-code platforms** like **ManyChat** offer free plans, but advanced features often require a paid subscription. **Low-code and AI-powered platforms** typically have tiered pricing based on usage, so it's important to factor in your budget when selecting a platform.

Step-by-Step Instructions for Setting Up a Basic Chatbot

Now that you have an idea of the platforms available, let's walk through the steps of setting up a simple chatbot using **ManyChat**, a popular no-code platform.

Step 1: Sign Up and Create a New Bot

1. Go to the **ManyChat** website and sign up for a free account.

2. Once logged in, click on "Create a New Bot" and choose the platform you want to integrate the bot with (e.g., Facebook Messenger).

3. You'll be prompted to connect your Facebook account. Once connected, select the Facebook page where you want to deploy your bot.

Step 2: Set Up Your First Conversation

1. After your page is connected, you'll be directed to the ManyChat dashboard. Click on "Automation" in the left-hand menu.

2. Click on "+ New Flow" to start building your chatbot's conversation.

3. Create a simple greeting message, such as: "Hello! How can I assist you today?"

4. Add response options like: "1. Get Help with Orders" and "2. Contact Support."

Step 3: Configure Responses and Actions

1. For each response option, you'll add corresponding actions. For example, if a user selects "Get Help with Orders," you can add an action to send a message like, "Please enter your order number."

2. You can also add **Quick Replies** (predefined responses) to make the conversation smoother.

Step 4: Test Your Chatbot

1. After configuring your chatbot, click on "Preview" to test how the chatbot interacts with users.

2. Use the built-in testing tool to simulate conversations and ensure the bot responds correctly.

3. Make any necessary adjustments to the flow and responses.

Step 5: Deploy and Monitor

1. Once you're satisfied with your chatbot, click "Publish" to make it live.

2. Monitor user interactions and track performance from the **Analytics** tab in ManyChat's dashboard.

Overcoming Common Beginner Challenges

While building a chatbot is more accessible than ever, beginners often face several challenges. Here are some tips to overcome them:

1. **Understanding User Intent**: One of the most common challenges is teaching your bot to understand user intent. Start with simple, clear questions and answers, and gradually build more complexity. **Dialogflow** offers **training tools** that help improve the bot's understanding over time.

2. **Creating Natural Conversations**: Making chatbots sound natural can be difficult. Focus on creating short, friendly messages that feel conversational. Test the chatbot's responses with real users to see if the tone is appropriate.

3. **Dealing with Limitations**: While no-code platforms are easy to use, they may lack some advanced features that experienced developers might need. Consider switching to a low-code or AI-powered platform like **Rasa** or **IBM Watson** if you require greater customization.

Choosing the right platform for building a chatbot depends on your goals, skill level, and the complexity of the chatbot you want to create. Whether you opt for no-code solutions like **Chatfuel** or **ManyChat**, low-code platforms like **Dialogflow**, or AI-powered tools like **ChatGPT**, there's a platform for every type of user. By following the steps outlined in this chapter and considering the tips provided, you'll be well on your way to creating your own chatbot and leveraging its power to automate tasks and enhance user experiences.

CHAPTER 3: DESIGNING CHATBOTS THAT ENGAGE AND CONVERT

Chatbots have become indispensable tools for businesses looking to streamline operations, enhance customer engagement, and drive conversions. However, the success of a chatbot hinges not only on its technical capabilities but also on how well it can engage users and guide them toward desired actions. Whether your goal is to increase sales, capture leads, or provide customer support, a chatbot must offer a seamless, engaging, and personalized experience.

This chapter provides a comprehensive guide to designing chatbots that not only engage users but also convert interactions into meaningful outcomes. We will explore the importance of conversational design, the best practices for crafting effective conversational flows, and strategies for personalizing user experiences. Furthermore, we will discuss methods for improving chatbot usability, optimizing user journeys, and testing chatbot performance to ensure maximum effectiveness. Lastly, we'll look at real-world case studies of successful chatbots to illustrate the principles discussed.

The Importance of Conversational Design

Conversational design refers to the art of structuring interactions between a user and a chatbot. Just as an engaging script is crucial for a successful customer service representative, well-crafted conversations are fundamental to a chatbot's effectiveness. The goal is to create dialogues that feel natural, intuitive, and lead users toward a specific outcome, whether that's making a purchase, signing up for a newsletter, or solving a problem.

Effective conversational design takes into account several factors:

1. **User Intent**: Understanding what the user is trying to achieve is the first step in designing a chatbot that works well. This requires anticipating common user queries and structuring responses accordingly.

2. **Tone and Language**: The tone should reflect your brand's personality. Is your brand formal or casual? Friendly or authoritative? The language and tone of the chatbot's responses should align with your brand's voice while also being easy for the user to understand.

3. **Ease of Use**: Simplicity is key. A chatbot should not overwhelm users with unnecessary options or information. Keeping interactions concise and straightforward will improve usability and satisfaction.

4. **Flow of Conversation**: The flow of conversation must be logical and intuitive. An effective flow guides the user from one step to the next, without confusion or delays.

Best Practices for Crafting Effective Conversational Flows

The structure and design of your chatbot's conversation flow are crucial for ensuring that users stay engaged and are motivated to complete actions. Here are some best practices to help you design a chatbot that engages users effectively:

1. **Start with a Friendly Greeting**

    o   A warm and welcoming greeting sets the tone for a positive interaction. For example, a chatbot could start with something like, "Hi there! How can I help you today?" instead of simply diving into a list of options.

    o   Personalized greetings, such as using the user's name if known, also help build rapport right from the start.

2. **Keep It Simple**

    o   The key to effective conversational design is simplicity. Offer a few clear options for users to choose from rather than overwhelming them with a wall of text.

    o   Use buttons, quick replies, and cards to make it easier for users to take action quickly, without needing to type out long responses.

3. **Guide the User Step-by-Step**

    o   A good chatbot will guide users through the interaction with minimal effort. If the user needs to perform a specific task (e.g., booking an appointment or purchasing a product), the chatbot should break the process into simple steps.

- For instance, instead of asking the user for a lot of information upfront, break down the request into smaller chunks: "Please provide your name," then "What date would you like to book for?" and so on.

4. **Use Personalization**

    - Personalization is one of the most effective ways to engage users. A chatbot that remembers past interactions and offers tailored recommendations will feel more intuitive and human-like.

    - For example, if a user has interacted with the chatbot before, the chatbot can say, "Welcome back! Would you like to pick up where you left off?"

5. **Provide Clear Options**

    - Always give users clear options to choose from to avoid confusion. If the chatbot is unsure of how to respond to a query, it should provide the user with options that could help guide the conversation in the right direction.

    - Use buttons for responses like "Yes," "No," or "I need help" rather than free-form text input, which can lead to misunderstandings.

6. **Offer Helpful Responses**
    - A chatbot must be able to handle a variety of scenarios and provide helpful responses. If the chatbot can't answer a question, it should direct the user to another resource, such as a human agent or relevant page on your website.

7. **Use Error Handling**
    - Despite the best planning, users will occasionally input something the chatbot doesn't understand. In such cases, it's essential to have error handling in place.
    - A good approach is to politely ask the user to rephrase their query or offer a set of options to guide them back on track.

8. **End with a Clear Call to Action**
    - Every interaction with a chatbot should aim toward a clear goal, such as making a purchase, submitting a form, or providing feedback. A strong call to action (CTA) should be included at the end of the conversation, such as "Would you like to complete your order?" or "Click here to talk to a live agent."
    - Providing a clear next step helps users feel confident about what to do next.

Strategies for Personalizing User Experiences

Personalization is essential for increasing engagement and conversion rates. The more a chatbot can tailor its responses to the user's specific needs, preferences, and behaviors, the more likely the user is to feel valued and understood.

Here are some strategies for personalizing user experiences:

1. **Use User Data Wisely**
     - If you collect data from users (such as their name, location, or past purchases), use it to tailor responses and provide more relevant recommendations. For example, a travel agency chatbot could ask, "Are you still planning your trip to Paris?" if it knows the user's previous interaction was about booking a trip there.

2. **Create Segmented Experiences**
     - Segment your audience based on various criteria, such as demographics, past behavior, or purchase history. This allows you to create personalized experiences for different groups of users. For example, a chatbot could offer personalized product recommendations based on a user's previous browsing history or recent interactions.

3. **Leverage AI and Machine Learning**

    o Advanced AI-powered chatbots can learn from each interaction, becoming better at understanding user preferences over time. Implementing machine learning algorithms will enable your chatbot to adapt to user needs and improve its responses.

    o For example, if a user frequently asks about a particular product, the chatbot can suggest related items or provide updates on the availability of the item.

4. **Use Contextual Information**

    o Contextualization is the ability of the chatbot to understand the user's situation and offer responses that are relevant in the moment. For instance, if a user is browsing an online store and adds an item to their cart, the chatbot could ask, "Would you like to proceed to checkout?"

Tips for Improving Chatbot Usability

A chatbot's usability directly impacts its ability to engage users and drive conversions. A poorly designed or difficult-to-use chatbot will frustrate users, leading to abandoned conversations and missed opportunities. Here are some tips for improving usability:

1. **Optimize for Speed**
    - Users expect quick responses from chatbots. Ensure that your chatbot responds promptly and avoids long delays between user input and the bot's response.

2. **Keep the Conversation Flow Smooth**
    - Ensure that the conversation flows naturally, with responses being coherent and relevant. A disjointed conversation will quickly lose the user's attention.

3. **Be Accessible Across Platforms**
    - Ensure that your chatbot is accessible across various platforms, whether it's on your website, social media, or mobile app. Users should be able to engage with the chatbot from wherever they are.

4. **Simplify Language**
    - Avoid using jargon or overly technical language in your chatbot's responses. The bot should speak in simple, easy-to-understand language to ensure that all users can interact with it effectively.

Testing Chatbot Performance for Better Results

Before deploying your chatbot, testing is crucial to ensure that it functions as intended. Regular testing also helps identify areas for improvement and fine-tuning.

1. **Test with Real Users**
    - Conduct user testing with real people to identify any issues with the chatbot's functionality or usability. Watch how users interact with the bot, and collect feedback on their experience.

2. **Monitor Analytics**
    - Track chatbot performance using analytics tools. Key metrics to monitor include completion rates, user satisfaction, conversion rates, and average response times. Use this data to make informed adjustments to improve the bot's performance.

3. **A/B Testing**
    - Perform A/B testing on different versions of your chatbot's dialogue to determine which conversation flows and responses lead to the best outcomes, whether that's a higher conversion rate or better user engagement.

Case Studies: Examples of Engaging and High-Converting Chatbots

1. **Sephora's Virtual Artist**
   o Sephora's chatbot, Virtual Artist, allows customers to try on makeup virtually using augmented reality. The bot provides personalized product recommendations based on the user's preferences, making the shopping experience more engaging and converting visitors into customers.

2. **H&M's Chatbot**
   o H&M's chatbot guides users through their shopping journey by suggesting products based on their style and preferences. It also sends personalized offers, encouraging users to make purchases.

3. **Macy's On-Call**
   o Macy's developed a chatbot to assist customers in navigating its large department stores. By using location-based technology, the chatbot can provide tailored directions, product information, and assistance, helping shoppers find what they need quickly and easily.

Designing a chatbot that engages users and drives conversions requires careful attention to conversational design, personalization, and usability. By following best practices for crafting clear and compelling conversations, personalizing user experiences, and optimizing chatbot performance, businesses can create chatbots that not only attract but also retain and convert customers. Regular testing and iteration are essential for ensuring that your chatbot remains relevant and effective, driving long-term success. The future of chatbot technology holds immense potential, and mastering the art of designing engaging, high-converting bots is key to staying ahead in the competitive landscape.

CHAPTER 4: ADVANCED FEATURES: ENHANCING CHATBOTS WITH GPT-4 AND AI TOOLS

Chatbots have evolved significantly over the past decade, transitioning from simple rule-based systems to highly advanced AI-driven conversational agents. With the advent of cutting-edge technologies like **GPT-4** and other artificial intelligence (AI) tools, the capabilities of chatbots have expanded exponentially. Today, chatbots can not only simulate human-like conversations but also perform complex tasks, understand natural language, and offer personalized interactions across multiple platforms.

This chapter delves into the integration of advanced features into chatbots using GPT-4 and other AI tools. We will explore natural language processing (NLP), multi-lingual capabilities, and cross-platform compatibility, all of which contribute to creating smarter, more intuitive, and efficient chatbots. Additionally, we will examine practical applications such as content generation, personalized recommendations, and dynamic responses, offering real-world examples and actionable tips for utilizing these tools effectively.

1. Natural Language Processing (NLP): Understanding and Improving Communication

Natural Language Processing (NLP) is at the core of advanced chatbot development. NLP enables chatbots to understand, interpret, and generate human language in a way that mimics natural conversation. With GPT-4, chatbots can process and respond to a wide array of questions, requests, and inputs in a highly sophisticated manner.

What is NLP?

NLP involves several subfields such as **tokenization**, **part-of-speech tagging**, **named entity recognition (NER)**, and **sentiment analysis**. These allow chatbots to perform tasks such as:

- **Breaking down sentences into smaller units**: Understanding words, phrases, and syntax to extract meaning.

- **Identifying intent**: Recognizing the user's objective behind a message.

- **Understanding context**: Acknowledging prior messages in a conversation to ensure relevance and coherence.

- **Sentiment analysis**: Determining whether the user's message is positive, negative, or neutral, which can guide how the chatbot responds.

GPT-4 and NLP Integration

GPT-4's superior NLP capabilities allow it to generate human-like text, making conversations more natural and fluid. By integrating GPT-4 into your chatbot, you can achieve:

- **Contextual Understanding**: GPT-4 has the ability to understand the context of a conversation, allowing it to deliver more relevant and accurate responses. For instance, it can refer back to prior exchanges and maintain the flow of the conversation.

- **Language Generation**: GPT-4 excels at generating coherent, natural-sounding responses to user queries, making it a perfect tool for enhancing chatbot conversations.

- **Multiturn Conversations**: Unlike simpler chatbots, GPT-4 can handle conversations involving multiple turns, enabling a back-and-forth dialogue that feels more like interacting with a human.

Practical Steps for Integrating NLP into Your Chatbot

1. **Choose an NLP API**: GPT-4's API, or other NLP tools such as Google Cloud NLP or Microsoft Azure Text Analytics, can be integrated into your chatbot framework. These tools offer pre-built capabilities like sentiment analysis, entity recognition, and text classification.

2. **Define the Chatbot's Purpose**: To optimize NLP integration, define the chatbot's primary use case (e.g., customer service, lead generation, etc.) and tailor the NLP configuration accordingly.

3. **Train the Model**: While GPT-4 offers powerful pre-trained models, training the system with specific industry terms, phrases, and company data can help refine responses for better accuracy.

4. **Handle Ambiguities**: Build fallback responses or handover mechanisms to human agents for situations where the chatbot cannot understand or resolve the query.

2. Multi-Lingual Capabilities: Bridging Language Barriers

In an increasingly globalized world, multi-lingual capabilities are essential for chatbots serving diverse user bases. With the power of GPT-4 and AI translation tools, chatbots can now converse in multiple languages, offering users personalized experiences regardless of their location or preferred language.

Importance of Multi-Lingual Capabilities

Having a chatbot that can understand and respond in multiple languages is crucial for:

- **Expanding Market Reach**: Businesses can provide support and engage with customers in various regions, effectively reaching a wider audience.

- **Improving User Experience**: By communicating in the user's native language, you enhance their experience and build trust.

- **Minimizing Frustration**: Language barriers can often lead to confusion and frustration. A multi-lingual chatbot can alleviate this by offering users seamless communication.

GPT-4 for Multi-Lingual Support

GPT-4's multilingual abilities are impressive. It supports a variety of languages and can understand context, tone, and meaning in these languages. Some notable features include:

- **Automatic Language Detection**: GPT-4 can detect the language of the user's input and respond in the same language, creating a seamless conversation flow.

- **Contextual Translation**: GPT-4 excels at context-aware translations, ensuring that idiomatic expressions or culturally specific phrases are translated accurately.

- **Language Switching**: The chatbot can switch between languages mid-conversation, catering to bilingual users or users who prefer to converse in different languages at different stages of the interaction.

Practical Steps for Implementing Multi-Lingual Features

1. **Identify Target Languages**: Decide which languages are most relevant to your audience. Use GPT-4's capabilities to cover these languages effectively.

2. **Integrate GPT-4 with Language Translation APIs**: If GPT-4's in-built translation capabilities are insufficient,

integrate third-party tools like Google Translate or Microsoft Translator for additional language support.

3. **Enable Language Switching**: Build mechanisms where users can manually switch languages during conversations, or automatically detect language preferences based on user profile settings.

4. **Test for Accuracy**: Run extensive testing to ensure that multi-lingual support works smoothly, with special attention to dialects, slang, and cultural nuances.

3. Cross-Platform Compatibility: Building a Unified Experience

Today, users interact with chatbots across multiple platforms, including websites, mobile apps, social media, and messaging apps. For a chatbot to be truly effective, it needs to offer a consistent and unified experience across all these touchpoints.

The Importance of Cross-Platform Compatibility

Cross-platform compatibility is essential for ensuring that your chatbot can reach users wherever they are. Whether users engage via Facebook Messenger, Slack, WhatsApp, or a website, the chatbot must provide consistent responses and user-friendly experiences. Moreover, maintaining consistent conversational context across platforms is crucial for the chatbot's effectiveness.

GPT-4 and Cross-Platform Integration

GPT-4's versatility allows for easy integration with multiple platforms. Using APIs, chatbots powered by GPT-4 can seamlessly operate across web pages, mobile applications, and third-party messaging services. For example:

- **Unified Conversation Context**: GPT-4 ensures that the chatbot retains context across multiple platforms, allowing users to start a conversation on one device (e.g., a smartphone) and continue it on another (e.g., a desktop).

- **Adapting to Platform-Specific Norms**: Depending on the platform, a chatbot may need to adjust its responses or format. For instance, a chatbot on Facebook Messenger may use quick reply buttons, while a web-based chatbot might provide longer, more detailed responses.

Practical Steps for Implementing Cross-Platform Compatibility

1. **Develop a Centralized Backend**: Create a centralized backend system where all user data, interactions, and responses are stored. This will enable the chatbot to track conversations across multiple platforms.

2. **Integrate with Third-Party Messaging Platforms**: Use APIs to integrate your chatbot with popular messaging platforms like WhatsApp, Facebook Messenger, and Slack.

3. **Optimize for Mobile and Desktop**: Ensure that the chatbot's interface adapts well to both mobile and desktop environments, maintaining a consistent user experience.

4. **Test Across Platforms**: Regularly test the chatbot on each platform to ensure the experience remains consistent and that platform-specific features are functioning as expected.

4. Advanced Use Cases: Content Generation, Personalized Recommendations, and Dynamic Responses

GPT-4's capabilities extend far beyond basic conversational tasks. By leveraging its powerful content generation features, chatbots can create engaging, dynamic, and personalized user experiences. Below, we explore some advanced use cases for enhancing chatbot functionality.

Content Generation

One of the standout features of GPT-4 is its ability to generate high-quality content. Chatbots equipped with GPT-4 can produce articles, product descriptions, FAQs, and even marketing copy on demand. This can be incredibly useful for businesses that require fresh content but lack the time or resources to generate it manually.

Example: A travel agency chatbot can create personalized itineraries based on a user's preferences, or an e-commerce chatbot can generate unique product descriptions for thousands of items in a catalog.

Personalized Recommendations

By analyzing user behavior, preferences, and past interactions, GPT-4 can generate personalized recommendations. This is particularly beneficial in retail, entertainment, and service industries where personalized suggestions can significantly boost conversion rates.

Example: An online clothing store's chatbot powered by GPT-4 can recommend outfits based on the user's style, past purchases, and current trends.

Dynamic Responses

GPT-4's ability to generate dynamic responses enables chatbots to engage users in real-time, adjusting their behavior and responses according to the context of the conversation. This makes the chatbot feel more human-like and capable of handling complex queries with ease.

Example: A customer service chatbot can dynamically change its tone or approach based on the user's sentiment, offering empathetic responses to frustrated customers and more casual replies to those simply seeking information.

The integration of GPT-4 and AI tools into chatbot development is unlocking new possibilities for businesses looking to improve customer interactions and drive conversions. By leveraging advanced features such as NLP, multi-lingual support, cross-platform compatibility, and dynamic content generation, developers can create smarter, more engaging chatbots that provide meaningful and personalized experiences.

As AI continues to evolve, the capabilities of chatbots will only grow more powerful, offering unprecedented opportunities for businesses to innovate and stay ahead of the competition. Whether you're building a chatbot for customer service, lead generation, or content creation, understanding how to integrate advanced AI tools like GPT-4 will be key to delivering exceptional user experiences and achieving your business goals.

CHAPTER 5: MONETIZATION STRATEGIES FOR CHATBOTS

As businesses increasingly turn to artificial intelligence (AI) to enhance customer engagement, improve operational efficiency, and provide personalized services, chatbots have emerged as powerful tools for driving business growth. However, beyond their role in enhancing customer interactions, chatbots also present significant opportunities for **monetization**. Whether you're a developer, entrepreneur, or business owner, understanding how to capitalize on the full potential of chatbots can create new revenue streams, boost sales, and enhance customer retention.

This chapter explores various monetization strategies for chatbots, focusing on how they can generate leads, increase sales, and drive customer loyalty. From subscription models to upselling opportunities, we will delve into actionable tactics for leveraging chatbot technology to boost profitability. Additionally, we will examine real-world examples of successful chatbot monetization, providing insights and inspiration for implementing these strategies in your own chatbot business or product.

1. Generating Leads with Chatbots

One of the most common and effective ways chatbots are monetized is through lead generation. Chatbots are excellent at capturing potential customers' interest and collecting valuable information that businesses can use for targeted marketing and sales efforts. This process can take place across multiple industries, from e-commerce and real estate to education and finance.

How Chatbots Generate Leads

1. **Instant Lead Capture**: Unlike traditional forms where users need to fill out fields and wait for confirmation, chatbots engage users immediately. They can ask questions in real-time, guide visitors through processes, and automatically collect contact details such as email addresses, phone numbers, and preferences.

2. **Qualifying Leads**: Chatbots can be programmed to ask qualifying questions, helping businesses gather critical information about a lead's interest, budget, or specific needs. This way, businesses can prioritize high-quality leads and pass them along to sales teams for follow-up.

3. **Data Collection for Follow-up**: With integrated customer relationship management (CRM) tools, chatbots can capture and store lead data, making it easier for businesses to follow up with prospects through email marketing campaigns, automated outreach, or personalized messages.

Examples of Lead-Generating Chatbots

- **Real Estate Chatbots**: Real estate companies can use chatbots to qualify leads by asking potential buyers about their preferences (e.g., location, budget, type of property). Once qualified, the chatbot collects contact information, setting the stage for further engagement.

- **E-commerce Chatbots**: In e-commerce, a chatbot might offer product recommendations based on a user's browsing behavior, and collect contact details to follow up with personalized offers or discounts.

By integrating chatbots into their websites or landing pages, businesses can effectively capture and nurture leads, ultimately converting them into paying customers.

2. Boosting Sales through Chatbot Interactions

Beyond lead generation, chatbots play a key role in **driving sales**. With the ability to engage customers in real-time and provide personalized recommendations, chatbots can significantly influence purchase decisions and increase conversion rates.

How Chatbots Drive Sales

1. **Product Recommendations**: One of the most powerful sales-driving features of chatbots is their ability to offer personalized product recommendations. By analyzing user behavior and preferences, chatbots can suggest products that match the user's tastes or needs. This can increase both the number of items sold and the overall value of each transaction.

2. **Seamless Checkout Process**: Chatbots can simplify the purchasing process by guiding customers through a smooth and easy checkout experience. They can provide payment

options, answer any questions about the product, and offer upsell or cross-sell opportunities to increase average order value.

3. **Real-Time Support and Assistance**: Chatbots can address any doubts or questions that arise during the shopping process, reducing cart abandonment rates and boosting sales. For example, if a customer hesitates due to a lack of information, the chatbot can immediately provide detailed product descriptions, reviews, or even customer service support.

4. **Limited-Time Offers and Discounts**: Chatbots can be programmed to present exclusive offers or time-sensitive discounts to users, urging them to take immediate action and complete a purchase. This creates a sense of urgency and can push users towards making a quick decision.

Examples of Sales-Boosting Chatbots

- **Sephora's Virtual Artist**: Sephora's chatbot helps users try out makeup virtually, recommending products based on their preferences and guiding them through the purchasing process.

- **H&M's Chatbot**: H&M's chatbot assists customers with product selection and style advice, boosting conversion rates and increasing sales by offering personalized shopping experiences.

By utilizing chatbots to engage users throughout their purchasing journey, businesses can significantly increase sales and customer satisfaction.

3. Subscription Models: Creating Recurring Revenue

Subscription models are another effective way to monetize chatbots, especially for businesses that offer ongoing services or content. This model generates consistent, recurring revenue while providing users with continuous value.

How Subscription Models Work with Chatbots

1. **Freemium Model**: Many businesses use the **freemium** model, where users are provided with basic chatbot features for free, but they must pay for premium features or additional functionalities. For example, a chatbot offering personal finance advice might provide free basic tips but charge for more in-depth, tailored financial guidance.

2. **Content Access**: For content-driven businesses, such as news outlets or e-learning platforms, chatbots can offer a subscription model where users pay for premium access to articles, videos, or courses. The chatbot can suggest content based on user interests and encourage sign-ups for a premium subscription.

3. **Service-Based Subscriptions**: Businesses offering regular services (such as meal plans, fitness programs, or wellness coaching) can leverage chatbots to manage subscriptions, automate renewals, and provide personalized

recommendations. Chatbots can handle payment processing, update user preferences, and ensure a smooth ongoing relationship with customers.

Examples of Subscription-Based Chatbots

- **AI-Powered Learning Platforms**: Platforms like Duolingo or Skillshare use chatbots to help users engage with lessons or content. Premium users can access additional resources, creating an ongoing subscription-based revenue stream.

- **Fitness Coaching Bots**: A fitness chatbot offering personalized workout plans and meal suggestions can operate on a subscription basis, providing users with continuous support in exchange for a monthly fee.

The subscription model helps businesses generate predictable, long-term revenue streams while offering users value that encourages them to stay engaged.

4. Upselling and Cross-Selling Opportunities

Chatbots excel at **upselling** and **cross-selling** by offering users additional products or services that complement their existing purchase or interaction. These strategies not only increase the average transaction value but also enhance the customer experience by providing more tailored recommendations.

How Chatbots Implement Upselling and Cross-Selling

1. **Upselling**: Chatbots can recommend premium versions of a product or add-ons that enhance the user's initial purchase. For example, if a customer is buying a laptop, the chatbot might suggest a higher-end model with additional features or accessories such as a carrying case or extended warranty.

2. **Cross-Selling**: Chatbots can identify opportunities to offer complementary products. For example, a customer purchasing a smartphone could be offered related items like screen protectors, chargers, or Bluetooth headphones.

3. **Personalized Suggestions**: By leveraging user data and behavior, chatbots can suggest products or services that are likely to resonate with the customer, based on their preferences and purchase history. This increases the chances of making additional sales.

Examples of Upselling and Cross-Selling Chatbots

- **Amazon's Alexa**: Through Alexa, Amazon uses upselling and cross-selling tactics effectively. For example, Alexa may suggest an upgraded version of a product the user is browsing, or recommend additional items like accessories.

- **Telecom Providers**: Telecom chatbots often use upselling by offering users the chance to upgrade their plans for better features, such as increased data or international calling packages.

By integrating upselling and cross-selling strategies into chatbot interactions, businesses can significantly increase their revenue per user while providing personalized recommendations.

5. Paid Features and Premium Services

Many chatbots can monetize through **paid features** or **premium services** that enhance the user experience. These paid features typically offer added functionality, such as deeper customization or more advanced AI capabilities, and can be integrated into a chatbot's workflow.

How Paid Features Work

1. **Advanced Functionalities**: Businesses can charge users for accessing advanced features such as personalized recommendations, faster response times, priority customer support, or premium content.

2. **Customization Options**: Chatbots offering customized services or experiences can charge for personalization, such as the ability to save user preferences, change the chatbot's voice, or create specialized workflows.

3. **Exclusive Content or Services**: Offering exclusive access to content or services through a chatbot can also serve as a paid feature. For example, a fitness chatbot may charge users for in-depth health tracking, customized meal plans, or exclusive workout sessions.

Examples of Chatbots with Paid Features

- **Cleo**: Cleo is a chatbot that helps users with budgeting and financial management. It offers basic budgeting advice for free but charges users for access to premium features, such as personalized spending insights and savings goals.

- **Replika**: Replika is an AI chatbot that offers a free version with limited interaction and a premium version with personalized conversations, customizations, and extra features for a subscription fee.

Paid features and premium services can generate substantial revenue while enhancing user satisfaction by providing valuable, exclusive experiences.

Monetizing chatbots presents businesses with numerous opportunities to generate revenue and boost profitability. Whether you're looking to generate leads, drive sales, offer subscription-based services, or implement upselling and cross-selling strategies, chatbots are powerful tools that can create new income streams.

By incorporating advanced monetization tactics such as paid features, premium services, and strategic partnerships, businesses can unlock the full potential of chatbot technology. Furthermore, the examples of successful chatbot monetization explored in this chapter demonstrate the effectiveness of these strategies and provide a roadmap for creating profitable chatbot-driven business models.

As chatbot technology continues to evolve, the monetization opportunities will only expand. Embracing these strategies can help businesses stay competitive, maximize ROI, and provide users with valuable, engaging experiences that encourage long-term customer loyalty.

CHAPTER 6: DEVELOPING APPS AROUND YOUR CHATBOTS

As chatbots continue to transform how businesses interact with their customers, they have evolved beyond simple tools for customer service and engagement. Today, chatbots are capable of powering entire applications that can perform a wide range of tasks, from personal assistance to e-commerce transactions and beyond. Transforming a chatbot into a standalone app offers exciting opportunities for both developers and entrepreneurs, as it provides a user-friendly, AI-driven solution that can be accessed on a variety of platforms.

This chapter will explore how to **develop applications around your chatbots**, covering everything from turning a chatbot into a mobile or web app, to integrating third-party APIs, ensuring platform compatibility, and scaling apps to meet user demands. Whether you're a developer looking to create an advanced app or a business owner seeking to enhance customer experience, this chapter provides practical guidance and strategies to create apps that effectively incorporate chatbot functionality.

1. Transforming a Chatbot into a Standalone App

A chatbot's ability to function seamlessly across various platforms makes it an excellent candidate for integration into mobile, web, and desktop applications. Transforming your chatbot into a standalone app involves several important steps to ensure that it can function autonomously while still delivering a high level of interaction and engagement.

Step 1: Choose the Right Platform for Your App

The first decision when developing an app around your chatbot is deciding whether to build a **mobile app, web app,** or **desktop application**. Each platform offers its own advantages and challenges:

- **Mobile Apps** (iOS and Android): Mobile apps are the most common way to integrate chatbots for a direct, on-the-go user experience. Chatbot apps can be integrated into messaging platforms, like Facebook Messenger or WhatsApp, or created as native apps on mobile devices. Tools like React Native or Flutter can help developers build apps that work on both iOS and Android with a single codebase.

- **Web Apps**: Web applications are ideal for reaching a larger audience without requiring users to download anything. They can be accessed through any browser and can offer rich, interactive chatbot experiences. Web apps can leverage chatbot integrations on websites, blogs, or e-commerce stores.

- **Desktop Apps**: Desktop applications can be used for more specialized use cases where the chatbot needs to run continuously without being interrupted. These apps can be ideal for businesses where chatbots serve as part of a larger workflow, such as productivity tools or customer service applications.

Step 2: Designing the User Interface (UI) and User Experience (UX)

While the core functionality of a chatbot app is based on its AI-powered conversation engine, the app's success depends heavily on its **user interface (UI)** and **user experience (UX)**. In this stage, the goal is to create a seamless, intuitive experience for the user that encourages engagement and maximizes ease of use.

- **Designing for Chatbot Interactions**: The chatbot's interface needs to feel natural and engaging. It's important to design an easy-to-read chat interface with buttons, quick replies, and rich media (like images, videos, or voice messages) that enhance the user experience.

- **Conversation Flow**: A successful chatbot app includes a carefully mapped-out conversation flow. The conversations should feel personal, responsive, and prompt, without overwhelming users with too much information. Consider how users will interact with the chatbot, what they need to achieve, and how the chatbot can guide them effectively.

- **Consistency**: The app should be visually consistent with your brand and maintain a clear, simple design that's easy to navigate. Minimalism often works best for chatbots, allowing users to focus on the conversation without distraction.

Step 3: Implementing the Chatbot Engine

The chatbot engine itself powers the interactions and provides the AI-driven conversation. You need to integrate the chatbot's conversation engine within your app framework. Depending on the complexity of your chatbot, you might use a pre-built engine, such as **Dialogflow**, **Microsoft Bot Framework**, or **Rasa**, or you may build a custom solution using a programming language like Python.

- **Natural Language Processing (NLP)**: Implementing NLP capabilities ensures that the chatbot understands and responds to user inputs in a conversational way. This technology allows the chatbot to analyze text input, identify user intent, and respond accordingly.

- **Real-Time Processing**: Ensure that the chatbot can process and respond to messages in real time, enhancing the responsiveness of the app. Users expect immediate interaction, so real-time message delivery and accurate responses are crucial to maintaining engagement.

2. Importance of APIs and Third-Party Integrations

A core element of building apps around chatbots is integrating third-party tools and APIs to enhance functionality and user experience. These integrations can connect the chatbot to external data sources, provide personalized recommendations, and enhance the overall value of the app.

What are APIs?

APIs, or **Application Programming Interfaces**, allow different software systems to communicate with each other. By leveraging APIs, developers can enhance their chatbot's capabilities by integrating external services, such as payment gateways, social media, customer databases, analytics, and more.

Popular API Integrations for Chatbot Apps

1. **Payment Gateways**: If your chatbot app supports e-commerce, integrating payment gateways such as **Stripe** or **PayPal** allows users to make purchases directly through the chatbot.

2. **Customer Relationship Management (CRM)**: Integrating with CRM systems such as **Salesforce** or **HubSpot** helps chatbots track customer interactions, provide personalized responses, and improve sales and marketing efforts.

3. **Calendar and Scheduling**: By integrating with tools like **Google Calendar** or **Calendly**, chatbots can help users

schedule appointments, meetings, or reminders directly through the app.

4. **Social Media and Messaging**: Integrating with social media platforms such as **Facebook Messenger**, **WhatsApp**, or **Telegram** allows the chatbot to provide cross-platform communication, ensuring that users can interact with the chatbot wherever they are.

5. **Analytics Tools**: By using tools like **Google Analytics**, **Mixpanel**, or **Chatbase**, developers can track user interactions with the chatbot, identify pain points, and gather insights to continuously improve the chatbot and app.

Benefits of API Integrations

1. **Enhanced Functionality**: APIs allow developers to add features that extend the capabilities of the chatbot, making it more useful and versatile for users.

2. **Faster Development**: Rather than building everything from scratch, APIs provide ready-made solutions for many common app features, allowing developers to focus on the core functionality of the chatbot.

3. **Scalability**: APIs help integrate the chatbot with services that can scale with user demands, whether that's through processing payments, handling large volumes of customer inquiries, or storing and retrieving data from external sources.

3. Developing Mobile and Web Apps for Chatbots

Creating a successful mobile or web app around your chatbot requires not only a strong AI foundation but also a deep understanding of development practices that ensure compatibility, responsiveness, and user satisfaction.

Best Practices for Developing Mobile Apps with Chatbot Functionality

1. **Cross-Platform Compatibility**: Mobile apps should be designed to work across both **iOS** and **Android** devices. Tools like **React Native** or **Flutter** enable developers to write a single codebase that works for both platforms, ensuring a wide reach.

2. **Push Notifications**: For ongoing engagement, integrate **push notifications** that alert users to new messages, updates, or special offers. This keeps users engaged with the chatbot even when they're not actively using the app.

3. **User Authentication**: For apps that require personal data or transactions, it's essential to implement **secure authentication** (e.g., OAuth, two-factor authentication). This protects user information and builds trust.

4. **App Performance Optimization**: Mobile apps should be optimized for **fast loading times** and **smooth interactions**. This includes optimizing chatbot responses,

reducing latency, and ensuring that the app works well on devices with different processing capabilities.

Best Practices for Developing Web Apps with Chatbot Functionality

1. **Responsive Design**: Ensure the chatbot interface works across various screen sizes. Use **responsive web design** to ensure that users can interact with the chatbot seamlessly on both desktops and mobile browsers.

2. **Web Hosting and Security**: Ensure that the web app is hosted on a secure server with proper SSL encryption. This ensures that all data exchanged between the user and the chatbot is secure and private.

3. **SEO and Discoverability**: If your web app is customer-facing and includes public-facing content, focus on **search engine optimization (SEO)** to ensure that your chatbot app ranks well on search engines and attracts traffic organically.

---

4. Scaling Your Chatbot App to Meet User Demands

As your chatbot app gains traction, it's important to prepare for **scalability**. Scaling your app to meet increased user demand involves both technical and operational considerations.

Technical Aspects of Scaling

1. **Server and Infrastructure Scaling**: As the number of users grows, you will need to ensure that your server infrastructure can handle the increased load. **Cloud services** like **AWS**, **Google Cloud**, or **Microsoft Azure** can provide auto-scaling to ensure your app performs well under heavy traffic.

2. **Database Scaling**: A growing user base means more data to process. Consider **sharding** or using a **distributed database system** to ensure your app can scale smoothly.

3. **Chatbot Optimization**: Continuously optimize the chatbot's NLP capabilities to handle increasing traffic and provide accurate responses to a wider range of user inputs.

Operational Considerations

1. **Customer Support**: As your chatbot app scales, it may be necessary to add live support options for users when the chatbot cannot address complex or specialized queries.

2. **User Feedback**: Solicit feedback from users to understand their pain points and identify areas for improvement, ensuring that the chatbot evolves with user needs.

Developing an app around your chatbot requires careful planning and a robust technical foundation. From transforming a chatbot into a fully-functional mobile or web app, to integrating third-party tools, ensuring compatibility, and scaling the app to meet user demands, the process involves both strategic and technical expertise. By following best practices in design, development, and optimization, you can create an app that not only integrates advanced chatbot functionality but also provides users with an exceptional experience that keeps them coming back.

As chatbot technology continues to evolve, the potential for developing innovative apps grows. By building apps around your chatbot, you can leverage the power of AI to solve real-world problems, enhance user experiences, and create scalable, profitable solutions that meet the demands of today's digital landscape.

CHAPTER 7: SCALING AND SUCCEEDING: BUILDING A CHATBOT EMPIRE

The world of chatbots has seen a dramatic transformation over the past decade, with businesses across various industries leveraging this technology to streamline customer service, boost sales, and increase engagement. However, the journey doesn't end with building an effective chatbot or a functional chatbot-driven app. To truly succeed, businesses need to scale their operations, refine their strategies, and ensure they stay competitive in an ever-evolving landscape dominated by advancements in artificial intelligence (AI).

In this chapter, we will explore how to **scale your chatbot business** for long-term success. From analyzing performance metrics to developing strategies for growth, client acquisition, and retention, we will provide actionable steps that help you build a sustainable **chatbot empire**. We will also discuss how to stay competitive in the rapidly changing AI industry and highlight real-world examples of chatbot businesses that have successfully scaled.

1. Understanding the Key Metrics for Analyzing Performance

Before you can scale your chatbot business, it's essential to understand how well your chatbot is performing. Performance metrics give you valuable insights into user behavior, operational effectiveness, and areas where improvements are needed. These insights will form the foundation of your scaling strategy.

Key Performance Indicators (KPIs) for Chatbots

1. **User Engagement Rate**: This is the measure of how actively users are engaging with your chatbot. Higher engagement rates typically indicate that your chatbot is providing value to your users. To measure engagement, track how many users initiate conversations, how long they stay engaged, and how many return for repeated interactions.

2. **Conversion Rate**: This metric tracks the percentage of chatbot interactions that lead to a specific desired outcome—whether that's making a purchase, scheduling an appointment, or signing up for a service. By understanding how well your chatbot is converting users, you can refine its performance and tailor its responses to boost conversion rates.

3. **Response Time and Accuracy**: Chatbots that respond quickly and accurately are essential for user satisfaction. Measure how long it takes for your chatbot to respond to inquiries and how accurate those responses are. Slow response times or poor accuracy can lead to user frustration and disengagement.

4. **User Retention Rate**: Retention is a critical indicator of your chatbot's long-term success. High retention rates

suggest that users find your chatbot valuable enough to come back. Measure how often users return to interact with your chatbot, and segment the data by user demographics or behaviors to find trends.

5. **Customer Satisfaction and Feedback**: Actively seek user feedback through post-conversation surveys or rating systems to gauge how satisfied users are with the chatbot. Customer satisfaction is crucial to building a long-term relationship with users and clients, so continuously monitor and improve based on feedback.

Analyzing Data for Continuous Improvement

Once you've established your KPIs, it's essential to consistently analyze and act on the data. For example, if your chatbot has a low conversion rate, you may need to tweak its conversation flow, offer additional prompts, or ensure it integrates effectively with a sales platform. Similarly, if users aren't returning, it might be a sign that the chatbot isn't providing enough ongoing value, and you'll need to introduce features or functionality that keep them engaged.

Data analysis tools like **Google Analytics**, **Mixpanel**, and **Chatbase** can help you gather and interpret user interactions and chatbot performance metrics, which will be vital in scaling your chatbot business effectively.

2. Strategies for Scaling Your Chatbot Operations

Scaling a chatbot business involves more than just increasing the number of users. It requires optimizing your operations, expanding your customer base, and ensuring that your chatbot can handle a larger volume of interactions without sacrificing performance or user experience.

A. Expanding Your Service Offerings

As your chatbot business grows, you will need to diversify and expand your offerings to meet the changing needs of your clients. Here are some strategies:

1. **Custom Solutions for Different Industries**: A one-size-fits-all chatbot solution may not appeal to every business. As you scale, consider tailoring your chatbot offerings for different industries, such as healthcare, finance, retail, or e-commerce. By customizing your chatbot's functionality to meet the specific needs of each industry, you can attract a broader client base.

2. **Multi-Channel Integration**: Scaling your chatbot means making sure it's accessible to as many users as possible. Consider integrating your chatbot into multiple channels such as social media (Facebook Messenger, WhatsApp, Instagram), websites, mobile apps, and even voice assistants like **Amazon Alexa** or **Google Assistant**. By expanding the reach of your chatbot, you open the door to more opportunities for user engagement and monetization.

3. **Advanced AI Features**: To remain competitive, you'll need to continue evolving your chatbot's capabilities. Consider adding advanced features like **sentiment analysis, multi-language support, personalization**, and **predictive analytics** to your chatbot. These features not only enhance user experience but also allow your chatbot to serve businesses in more complex ways, opening up new avenues for growth.

B. Building an Efficient Infrastructure

As the user base and interactions with your chatbot increase, so will the demand for computational resources. To ensure your chatbot scales effectively, invest in infrastructure that can support growth:

1. **Cloud Hosting**: Use cloud services like **AWS, Google Cloud**, or **Microsoft Azure** to scale your infrastructure as needed. These platforms offer flexible scaling options, which can automatically adjust to fluctuations in traffic, ensuring that your chatbot can handle more users without downtime.

2. **API Integrations**: For scalable operations, you will likely need to connect your chatbot to other services and systems, such as customer relationship management (CRM) tools, databases, payment gateways, and more. Ensure that your chatbot is integrated with the right APIs to allow smooth interaction between systems and expand your operational capabilities.

3. **Data Storage and Management**: As your chatbot gathers more data, efficient data management becomes crucial. Ensure that your database can handle increased traffic and store data securely. Implement strategies for **data security** and **compliance** with industry regulations (such as GDPR) to protect your users' privacy.

3. Marketing Your Chatbot Business for Growth

Once you've built a robust chatbot, the next step is to scale your business through effective marketing strategies. With the chatbot industry becoming more competitive, marketing is crucial for client acquisition, retention, and brand recognition.

A. Client Acquisition Strategies

1. **Targeted Content Marketing**: Share educational content such as blog posts, videos, case studies, and infographics that demonstrate the benefits and success stories of your chatbot. Focus on industries and sectors that can benefit the most from your solution.

2. **Referral Programs**: Implement a referral program where your current clients can refer new customers to your chatbot services in exchange for rewards or discounts. Word-of-mouth marketing remains one of the most effective ways to grow a business.

3. **Paid Advertising**: Leverage digital advertising channels such as **Google Ads, Facebook Ads,** or **LinkedIn Ads** to target businesses looking for chatbot solutions. A well-targeted paid advertising campaign can help you reach decision-makers in industries that need chatbots.

4. **Partnerships and Collaborations**: Partner with other businesses that offer complementary services, such as web developers, digital marketing agencies, or CRM solution providers. These partnerships can help you tap into new customer bases and build long-term relationships.

B. Retention Strategies

Client retention is essential for sustaining growth and building long-term relationships. Here are some strategies to keep your clients happy:

1. **Offer Ongoing Support**: Provide top-tier customer support to help clients with any issues they encounter while using your chatbot. Regular check-ins and follow-ups can also help you identify problems early and address them before they escalate.

2. **Continuous Improvement**: Make sure your chatbot evolves with the changing needs of your clients. Regularly update your chatbot with new features, integrations, and optimizations based on client feedback and technological advancements.

3. **Customer Training**: Offer your clients training and resources to help them use your chatbot effectively. Providing educational materials, such as video tutorials or live demos, can increase their satisfaction and ensure they get the most value from your chatbot.

4. Staying Competitive in the Evolving AI Landscape

The chatbot and AI industries are constantly evolving, and staying competitive requires adaptability and a forward-thinking approach. Here are some strategies to maintain your competitive edge:

A. Embrace Emerging Technologies

1. **Voice-Activated Chatbots**: Voice technology is on the rise, with more users adopting voice assistants like **Siri**, **Alexa**, and **Google Assistant**. Consider incorporating voice recognition and natural language processing (NLP) into your chatbot to create voice-activated solutions that appeal to a broader audience.

2. **Machine Learning and AI Models**: Continuously update your chatbot's machine learning models to improve its understanding of user behavior and intent. By leveraging advancements in AI, you can make your chatbot more intelligent and responsive to user inputs.

3. **Automating Processes**: As businesses increasingly rely on automation, integrating your chatbot with enterprise tools

like **Salesforce**, **Zendesk**, and **Slack** can help automate workflows and provide seamless communication between different business functions.

B. Focus on Personalization

Personalization is key to staying ahead in the chatbot space. Develop chatbots that deliver highly personalized experiences based on user behavior, preferences, and past interactions. This could include personalized recommendations, tailored responses, and customized offers to improve user satisfaction and engagement.

---

5. Real-World Examples of Successful Chatbot Businesses

1. **Drift**: Drift is a leader in the conversational marketing space, helping businesses engage customers through AI-powered chatbots. Their chatbot platform is widely adopted by businesses looking to automate lead generation and qualification. Drift's success lies in its focus on **personalization** and its ability to integrate with CRM systems.

2. **Ada**: Ada provides an AI-powered customer service chatbot platform for enterprises. The company scaled its chatbot offerings by tailoring its technology to the needs of various industries, from healthcare to retail, and offering strong analytics and integrations with other business tools.

3. **Intercom**: Intercom's customer support chatbot has become a staple for businesses seeking to streamline customer communication. Their platform offers advanced features, including chatbots that can handle inquiries, trigger marketing messages, and automate ticketing systems.

Scaling a chatbot business requires more than just expanding your user base. It involves optimizing performance, enhancing features, and ensuring that your chatbot remains competitive in a fast-evolving industry. By understanding the metrics that matter, developing efficient operational strategies, and implementing effective marketing and retention strategies, you can build a successful chatbot empire.

Staying ahead in the AI landscape means embracing emerging technologies, focusing on personalization, and continuously evolving your chatbot to meet the demands of businesses and users alike. By learning from successful chatbot businesses and applying these insights to your own operations, you can scale your chatbot business and establish it as a leader in the AI-driven future.

www.ingramcontent.com/pod-product-compliance
Lightning Source LLC
Chambersburg PA
CBHW020456220526
45464CB00002B/1009